Later Elementary

Seasonal Scenes
AT THE PIANO

by Naoko Ikeda

CONTENTS

ISBN 978-1-4950-0256-4

WILLIS MUSIC

EXCLUSIVELY DISTRIBUTED BY

HAL•LEONARD®
CORPORATION

7777 W. BLUEMOUND RD. P.O. BOX 13819 MILWAUKEE, WI 53213

Visit Hal Leonard Online at
www.halleonard.com

FROM THE COMPOSER

Do you have a favorite season?

Think of this collection as five short animated stories in Winter, Spring, Summer, and Autumn. ("Prelude Perennial" can be played any time of the year, whenever you want to feel energized and refreshed.)

I invite you to experience the seasons with me.

Naoko Ikeda

PERFORMANCE NOTES

VELVET WINTER
It is the coldest winter imaginable, and a swan unfurls its wings quietly in the light of snow. It is white and cold, but there is warmth.

SPRING BREEZE
This is a conversation between the beautiful spring breeze and a field of green grass. Spring is here!

PRELUDE PERENNIAL
Here are four fairies, one for each season: the Winter Fairy, the Spring Fairy, the Summer Fairy, and the Autumn Fairy. In measures 1-4, the first fairy opens the door and ushers its season in with clear, crisp ascending arpeggios. The second follows in measures 5-8, the third in 9-12, and finally the fourth fairy in 13-16.

WAITING FOR SUMMER
Picture the ocean, with clear blue skies above. Swaying on the waves, a mermaid is busy making summer plans with her friends.

MARCH OF THE JACK-O'-LANTERNS
It is the middle of a moonlit autumn night, and hundreds of jack-o'-lanterns blink on and off. The little lanterns march forward when they are brave, but hop backwards every time they are afraid. Play with courage and determination.

Velvet Winter

for Naoe Ishimine

Naoko Ikeda

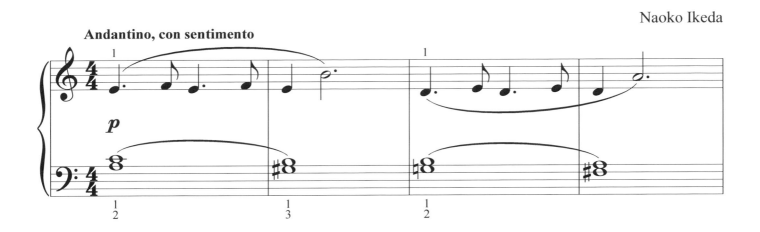

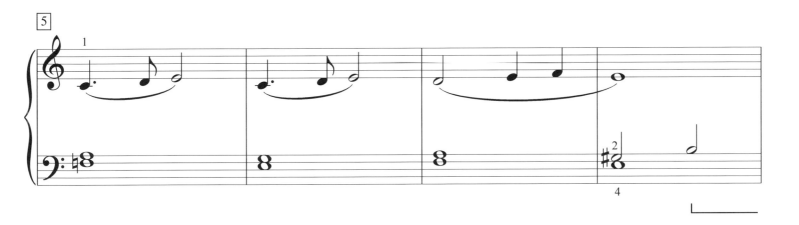

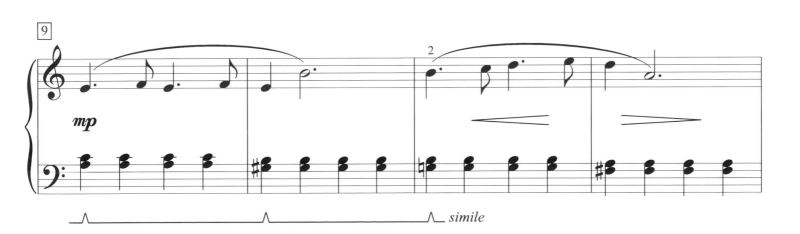

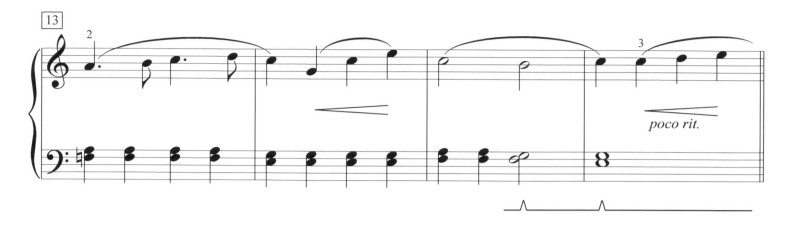

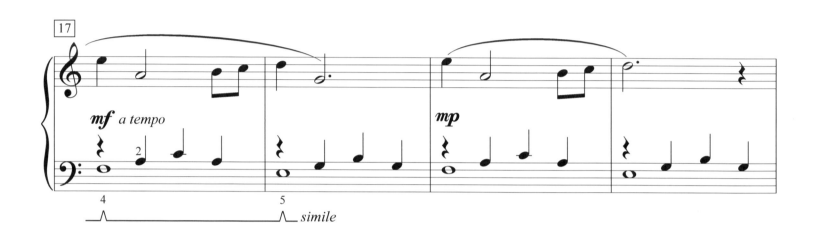

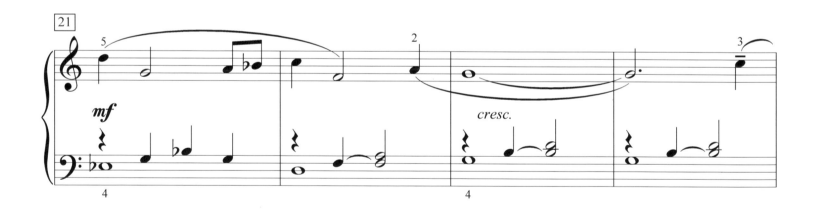

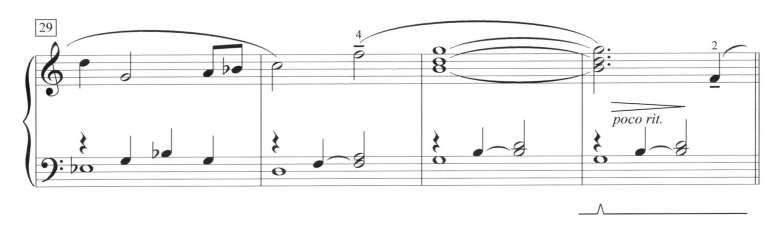

Spring Breeze

Naoko Ikeda

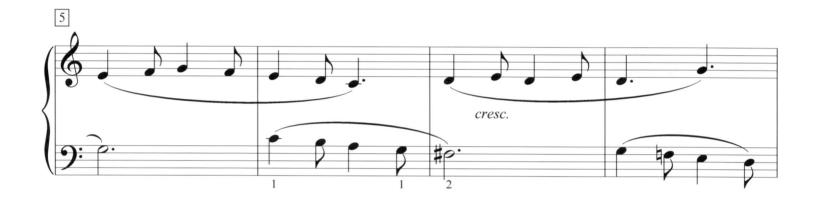

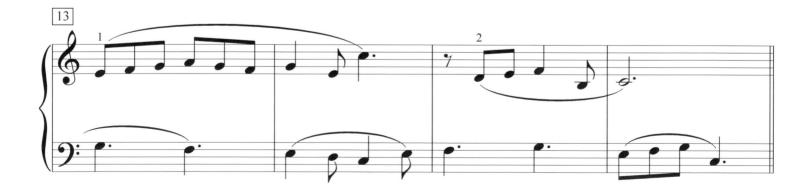

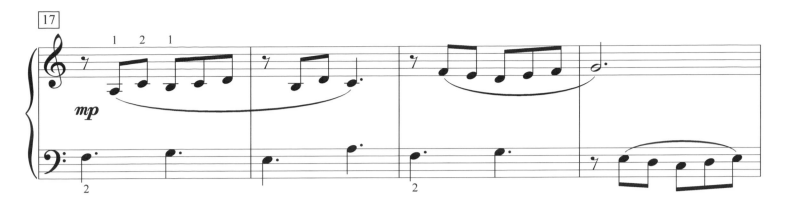

Prelude Perennial

for Mami Imano

Naoko Ikeda

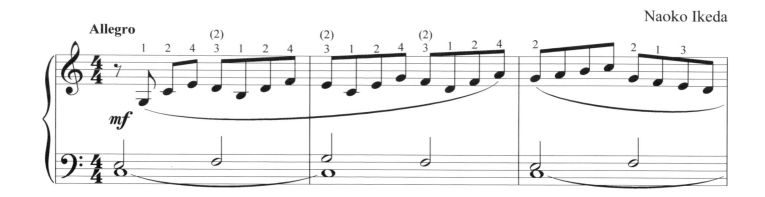

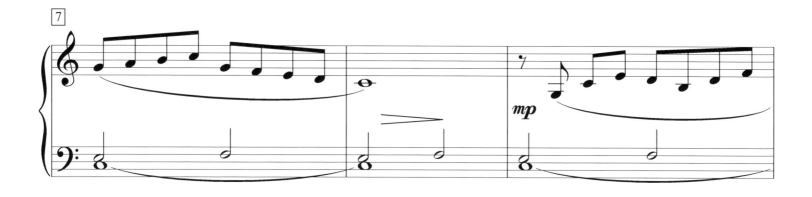

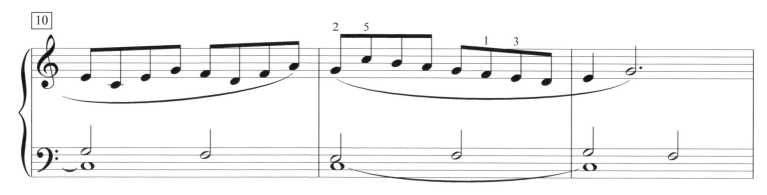

Waiting for Summer

for Michika Sakamoto

Naoko Ikeda

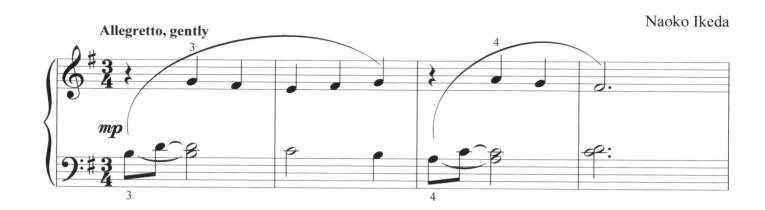

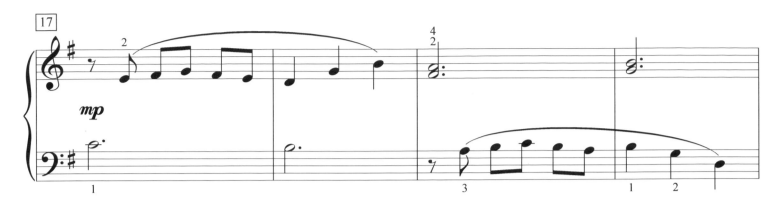

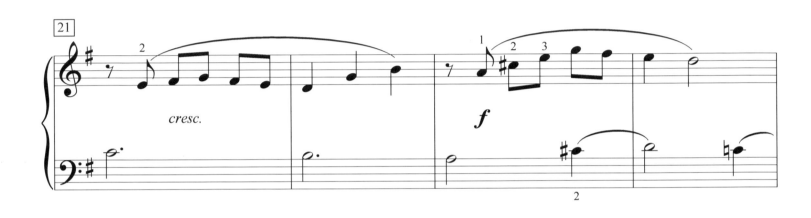

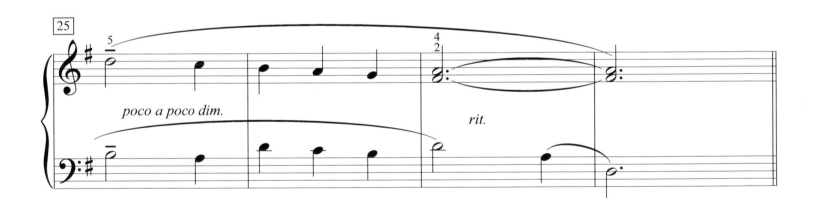

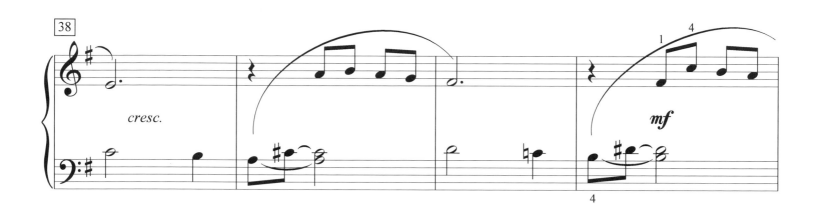

March of the Jack-o'-Lanterns

Naoko Ikeda

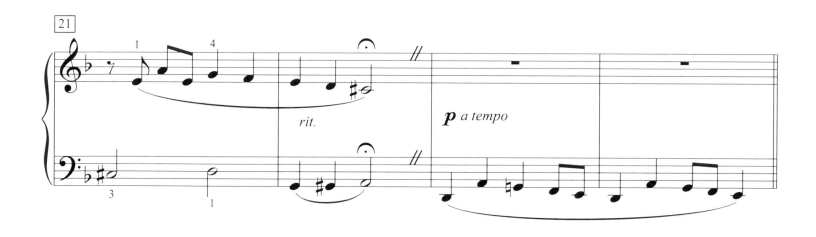

COMPOSER'S CHOICE

FROM WILLIS MUSIC

The Composer's Choice series showcases piano works by an exclusive group of composers, all of whom are also teachers and performers. Each collection contains classic piano pieces that were carefully chosen by the composer, as well as brand-new compositions written especially for the series. The composers also each contributed helpful and valuable performance notes for each collection. Get to know a new Willis composer today!

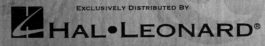
ELEMENTARY

COMPOSER'S CHOICE – GLENDA AUSTIN
8 Original Piano Solos
MID TO LATER ELEMENTARY LEVEL
Betcha-Can Boogie • Jivin' Around • The Plucky Penguin • Rolling Clouds • Shadow Tag • Southpaw Swing • Sunset Over the Sea • Tarantella (Spider at Midnight).
00130168 .... $6.99

COMPOSER'S CHOICE – CAROLYN MILLER
8 Original Piano Solos
MID TO LATER ELEMENTARY LEVEL
The Goldfish Pool • March of the Gnomes • More Fireflies • Morning Dew • Ping Pong • The Piper's Dance • Razz-a-ma-tazz • Rolling River.
00118951 .... $6.99

COMPOSER'S CHOICE – CAROLYN C. SETLIFF
8 Original Piano Solos
EARLY TO LATER ELEMENTARY LEVEL
Dark and Stormy Night • Dreamland • Fantastic Fingers • Peanut Brittle • Six Silly Geese • Snickerdoodle • Roses in Twilight • Seahorse Serenade.
00119289 .... $6.99

INTERMEDIATE

COMPOSER'S CHOICE – GLENDA AUSTIN
8 Original Piano Solos
EARLY TO MID-INTERMEDIATE LEVEL
Blue Mood Waltz • Chromatic Conversation • Etude in E Major • Midnight Caravan • Reverie • South Sea Lullaby • Tangorific • Valse Belle.
00115242 .... $8.99

COMPOSER'S CHOICE – ERIC BAUMGARTNER
8 Original Piano Solos
EARLY TO MID-INTERMEDIATE LEVEL
Aretta's Rhumba • Beale Street Boogie • The Cuckoo • Goblin Dance • Jackrabbit Ramble • Journey's End • New Orleans Nocturne • Scherzando.
00114465 .... $8.99

COMPOSER'S CHOICE – RANDALL HARTSELL
8 Original Piano Solos
EARLY TO MID-INTERMEDIATE LEVEL
Above the Clouds • Autumn Reverie • Raiders in the Night • River Dance • Showers at Daybreak • Sunbursts in the Rain • Sunset in Madrid • Tides of Tahiti.
00122211 .... $8.99

COMPOSER'S CHOICE – CAROLYN MILLER
8 Original Piano Solos
EARLY INTERMEDIATE LEVEL
Allison's Song • Little Waltz in E Minor • Reflections • Ripples in the Water • Arpeggio Waltz • Trumpet in the Night • Toccata Semplice • Rhapsody in A Minor.
00123897 .... $8.99